Transform Your Bu:
be Derailed

Learn how to take your business from
Incubation, fluttering, and flying to **Soaring**!

Be able to keep an eye on the details (from a
distance) and soar above the crowd!

Keep your business on track and heading in
the right direction.

Contents

Forward 3

Introduction 5

Who is the Engineer? 20

How is Your Vision?..25

Light at the End of the Tunnel............................38

All Aboard..45

On the Right Track..68

Do You Have a Caboose? 72

Who is Feeding the Engine?..................................80

Compartmentalized 91

At Your Service...96

Bridge Out...113

All Systems Go...123

Know Destination...137

Stop at the Depot 143

In Conclusion 150

About Soaring Eagles Business Advisors.......162

Forward

The book is for business owners and managers who want to grow the business beyond where it is currently. They want to strive towards a future and move their business to the next stage.

They seek to bring their talents, knowledge, experience, and abilities to their ideal target market. Your business is a driving force in our economic future. Your dedication and passion for your business are an example for others to admire.

You have decided that you need to keep your business on the right track but others may be trying to sidetrack your business. You have decided to not let others derail your plans and vision for your business. You are searching for ways to help your team to see the light at the end of the tunnel and where the business is headed. You may have been sitting at a standstill for some time and want to make sure you are heading in the right direction. There are so many options and you don't know where to start.

The purpose for this book is to provide you will valuable insights, strategies, and actions you can use to reach your destination for your business and personal life. As a business owner you have enjoyed engineering the start of your business but may feel like the business has become stagnant and not moving forward. You remember being excited about your initial vision for the business and the future.

We are committed to helping you to be strategic and passionate about the growth of your business and it's suppliers and customers or clients. We hope that you find this book and the ideas to be of great value to you and your business.

To the reader, we wish you the best of success!

Most sincerely,
Steven J. Beaman, CPBC - APBC

Follow us online:

Website: www.soaringeagleba.com
Facebook:
www.facebook.com/soaringeaglesba
Twitter: @stevenbeaman

Introduction

"There is nothing so useless as doing efficiently that which should not be done at all." - Peter Drucker

Do you feel stuck in your business in one of these areas?

You are working more hours than you would like.

You are unable to take time off, as you know the business cannot function without you.

You have inconsistent income.

You have a few systems and processes, but they are time consuming.

You feel that there isn't anyone who you can confide in.

You are not having fun in your business like you had envisioned when you started it.

You have all of your eggs in one basket (need more clients or customers).

You have a few goals but they are not written down or specific.

You have an inconsistent marketing strategy.

You don't know if your marketing is effective

And more …

If any of this describes you and your business, let me assure you that you are NOT alone.

It is very common for business owners to feel stuck. You have the knowledge and willingness to work on your business, but you just don't seem to find the time or the energy to work **ON** the business. You spend all or most of your time working **IN** the business.

You are already working long hours to make ends meet and do not have anyone else to turn to. Are you feeling like you are the only person trying to solve the issues?

Are you trying to do it all alone?

You may be headed for a derailment in your business.

In a business myself, I found that I was working long hours and still trying to have a consistent cash flow. I would get up in the morning and wonder what I should do first. I would work on different projects throughout the day.

At the end of the day, I would wonder what I had actually accomplished. This was not the case, but it can feel lonely at the top. I have seen this same scenario many times with businesses I have worked with. Does this sound like you?

You may need to develop more effective processes and systems that will allow your business to function more efficiently.

You would like to have more time for hobbies or other interests.

You would like to be able to spend more time with your family and friends without always being plugged into the business.

You would like to have all your people on the same track and pulling in the same direction.

You have multiple streams of income so that you can have a more consistent cash flow.

You may be paying yourself last after all your other expenses, if and when there are funds available. You see money going out faster than it is coming in.

Statistics show that 85% of businesses close within the first 5 years. In about the time it took you to read this statement, another business has closed its doors. Why? Because many business owners fail to plan, focus, and create the necessary systems and processes to generate sustainable growth. As a result, they suffer from fatigue, burn out, and lack of sustainable income.

Remember that behind every failed business there are unfulfilled dreams and aspirations of an owner who had hoped for a much different outcome for their endeavor. The impact on the owner and his or her family can often be very devastating. Financial issues, stress, marital conflict, and depression are just a few of the symptoms business owners often share. **It doesn't have to be this way!**

In this book, we will cover actions you can take to help your business move to the next stage of the business lifecycle.

You will learn steps you can take today to reach your destination and to follow your plan. You will learn actions you can take to be able to keep your business on track.

You can look forward to being able to build the kind of life and business you have always envisioned. Whether your business is doing well and simply seeking to improve or you feel stuck, this book can help!

The determining factor will be whether or not you decide to implement the ideas that are relevant to your situation and your willingness to take action.

Knowledge without action is folly.

Knowledge = Wisdom?

"The true delight is in the finding out rather than in the knowing." Isaac Asimov

Knowledge by itself does not lead to wisdom.

Today we live in an age of information overload as you can obtain so much knowledge using the internet, social media, electronic books, and other resources. Who knows what will be available for you in the future to gain more knowledge.

If knowledge alone translated into wisdom than we would all be wise beyond our years. We all know that this is not true and that wisdom is gained by applying the knowledge. We have to understand what we have been taught.

Wisdom is also gained from the failures or mistakes that we make along the way. It is not instantly apparent, but it is a virtue to be gained over time.

So what is missing when you have gained knowledge? It is the lack of taking ACTION or applying what you know to be true. You also "DO NOT KNOW, WHAT YOU DO NOT KNOW".

It's what you do with the knowledge you acquire that leads to wisdom or it is folly. If you don't apply the knowledge by taking action, it will remain a source of missed opportunities.

Imagine that you are sitting at a coffee shop and you decide you want a bagel with your drink. The solution to your situation is within reach of your feet. All you need to do is put your feet on the ground, and make your way to the counter so you can order your bagel. But until you actually get up and move your feet and take action, you stay in the same position and contemplate the bagel. Therefore, you have essentially stayed in the same place and are watching everyone enjoying his or her bagel.

Wayne Gretzky once said, **"You miss 100 percent of the shots you don't take"**.

Without taking deliberate action and applying what you know and moving your feet or stretching your mind nothing of great value will be accomplished.

Education + Application = Wisdom

Education by definition is the gaining of knowledge, skill, and understanding. Just having a skill does not mean that you are educated, you also need to understand how to use the skill and the knowledge of when and how to apply it.

Franchises have systems that allow the franchisee to follow a proven method for running their business.

Independent business owners do not have a set method for running their business so many times the processes and systems have to be created. You can use what someone else is doing, but is it really the right method or process for your business?

What makes your business different than your competition? What makes your business unique? What is your passion or your why for being in business?

Many business owners believe that by reading the latest or most current business articles or books or attending seminars, webinars, or workshops they will find the missing ingredients to their business success.

I see many business owners who are struggling or overwhelmed with information overload.
You may convince yourself that if you gain enough knowledge and information about running your business, it will be a success.

In one of my businesses, I had spent too much time getting ready to get ready.

What does success look like to you and your business?

Gaining knowledge is definitely important and very advisable. Be a life-long learner. You can never gain enough knowledge as the information is always changing. It is like trying to hit a moving target.

As an Information Technology Consultant for over 40 years, I have seen firsthand how quickly technology changes and how difficult it is to keep up.

Make sure you also spend time to broaden your perspective by what you are reading. Read a good business fiction book for some insight.

Readers are leaders and leaders are readers.

Learning a skill or talent does not necessarily mean that you understand the best ways to use it. The reality is that all of the education, knowledge, and information available in this world are folly without taking action on what you know to be true.

TAKE ACTION and APPLY!

The keys to success in any business are not as far off as you may think. It is not a hidden treasure you have to find, but there is a map that can take you there.

By focusing your attention on some key business fundamentals and processes, along with a trusted advisor who can provide support and encouragement to help you apply them in your business, you will see yourself making great strides to increase cash flow, profits, and the treasure you may be seeking.

Where your treasure is, there will your heart be also.

You may want to ask yourself this question:

"What are the key fundamentals and processes that I am working on in my business today?

What am I going to take action on today?

What action steps can I take today to move towards my ideal vision for my business?"

Rather than buying another business book, attending another networking event or seminar, maybe you should consider applying the education you already have acquired. The best place to start is often the last concept or tactic that was left incomplete.

Do you have a strategy for how to market your business for the best return on your investment of time and money?

Maybe you can put together some actions you need to take prior to, during, and after an event or conversation with a customer or client.

Do you periodically interview your customers or clients to see what they need?

In this life, many people know what to do, but many people do not actually apply what they know. Just knowing isn't enough! You must understand it and take action.

This book is not a be all and end all; you need to keep expanding your education. You need to pay close attention to the processes and ideas that may provide you with the highest possible return to produce the transformation in your business.

Be not conformed to this world, but be transformed by the renewing of your mind.

Application without Education = Failure

If "education + application = wisdom" and "application without education = failure", please consider the following true story.

As an employee for a manufacturing business working in their Information Technology area I made a decision to leave the business and start my own consulting business. Thankfully the manufacturing business hired me back as a consultant. They provided the only income for my business for a time.

A recruiting business found my resume on a website. They contacted me about a full time contract with a business in the area. The contract work lasted for 4 years. When the contract ended I had to start looking for more work. Thankfully I had saved some of the income from the full time contract. I did not know when the contract would end.

As a new business owner I took action without the education, which led to inconsistent income.

Many business owners fall into the same trap, which is why we see so many businesses that fail. They take action prior to gaining the necessary and critical education to succeed.

Many people may admire the business owner who just says, **"go for it"**, but the most successful business owners are those that have a plan and follow through on their plan. They are willing to adjust the plan in order to move the business forward towards their vision and goals.

True success is in the eye of the beholder.

They are able to stay on track and move their business to the next stage.

What is true success to you?

You can also get stuck in analysis paralysis with always learning and not applying it.

What is ACTION?

Acknowledge the situation – What is the roadblock?

Clarify the options – What option do I have?

Take advice – seek out qualified advisors who see the roadblock coming

Implement the action steps – Remove the roadblock or change direction?

Ongoing evaluation – Did the action or ideas resolve the situation?

Note the outcome – Was it resolved? If not, return to the Acknowledge step.

"Nothing happens without ACTION."

As you contemplate and ponder each idea and tactic in this book, determine where your business is at on a scale of 1 – 10, with 10 being the highest.

It is our hope that you take this seriously and that you become inspired and encouraged to move your business to the next stage in the business lifecycle.

You can also visit our website and take the Business Lifecycle Challenge to get an idea of where your business is on the Business Lifecycle.

Are you incubating, fluttering, flying, or soaring?

What stage is your business at or going through?

You are ready and wanting to break out of your shell.

You are thinking it is time to hire an advisor.

You are feeling Stuck in your business with nowhere to turn.

You are spending all of your time IN the business.

Let's get started to get your business **Soaring** and reaching the vision you had when you started your business.

It is possible when you take the initiative to go beyond status quo and to overcome your seemingly mountainous roadblocks.

Who is the Engineer?

"Begin with the end in mind." *– Peter Drucker*

"Your time is limited, so don't waste it trying to live someone else's life." = *Steve Jobs*

You have an operations manager or COO who keeps an eye on the details of the business and makes sure everything is in order. You provide him or her with the tools and resources they need to help you as the business owner to feel confident in their abilities. You are able to trust them with providing direction for the business without you having to consistently ask them about the business status.

You periodically meet with your top advisors to share your vision and to determine what might get in the way. You are able to keep the pulse of the company because you have dependable and trustworthy operations staff.

Who is the engineer in your business?

Is it you or do you allow others to share in the direction of the business?

You are able to delegate high level strategies and objectives to your operations team and are confident that they will do an exceptional job.

You don't intervene and throw a switch in the middle of the initiative unless it means that following the current track there will be a derailment of your business vision, mission, and values. You don't want to just blindly follow a strategy that is not working.

Your processes and systems support your operations so that there is no doubling of the information that is shared in your business. Your information is accurate and concise and is the same in multiple views. One of the sayings in Information Technology consulting that I have used is the idea of Garbage IN, Garbage Out (GIGO). If the information put in is inaccurate than the information received is inaccurate. It only stands to reason.

You know this to be true, but may find areas of your business where this principle is lacking. Do you have multiple processes and systems that contain the same information? You know that this is the case but may have chosen to ignore it or decided it wasn't worth the effort or expense to correct it. What is it really costing your business?

You can turn this situation around by focusing on Great Information IN, Great Information OUT or as I would call it (GIIGIO).

What is great information?

I would suggest that the best information is the information that allows the business to move forward. The information is critical for the business to make decisions and look towards the future not just the present.

Have information that forecasts the future revenue for the business. Create budgets for each area of the business that are realistic and measureable, just like you would for goals.

Many businesses focus on what a particular group of people need for information and they create their own silos of information.

They buy software and systems that do not interact with each other. Therefore, one system or process may produce a different outcome than another.

As an example, let's say that you have a marketing department that uses a process or system to track prospects and what they are looking for.

The sales department has a completely different system or process for tracking what the prospects bought after they became a customer or client.

The two processes or systems are not interacting so they each have different information. The marketing department continues to market a different product or service that the customer or client is not really interested in.

Now what will you do?

By sharing information in a customer or client relationship management process or system you are able to share the information across all areas of your business (Great IN, Great OUT).

This eliminates having your people trying to find someone that knows the answers to what a customer or client has purchased in the past.

It can also eliminate asking the same questions that the customer or client has already answered.

This system also enables your business to determine if a client or customer would likely purchase a complementary product or service. Your business may be considering carrying another product or service that would benefit your current customers or clients. In order to determine if the new product or service is viable for your business, you would be able to determine possible prospects more easily.

Connect with people who have been in your shoes or have succeeded in reaching their dream. Have people in your circle of influence that may have the answers, since you know that you don't have all the answers. Treat other people the way that you want to be treated. Be a positive influence in your business and with your customers or clients and suppliers.

How is Your Vision?

"The best way to predict the future is to invent it." *- Alan Kay*

"Take advantage of every opportunity to practice your communication skills so that when important occasions arise, you will have the gift, the style, the sharpness, the clarity, and the emotions to affect other people." *– Jim Rohn*

Do you have a clear vision for your business? Can you see beyond the day-to-day issues in your business? Is your business a real business or is it busyness?

Just like a train has to have a clear track with no obstacles getting in the way, so your business must have a clear vision of where it is going and how you are going to get there.

You need to have a clear mission, vision, and values in order for everyone in your business to be excited and engaged in your business. Without it you and your business can easily get off track and be heading in the wrong direction or worse yet be derailed.

Many business owners create a mission statement that they frame and post on the walls of their business. Many of these mission statements are rarely read or many times not even followed by the people in the business.

Many of the mission statements I have seen lack clarity as to what the mission really means.

The wording is similar to many other businesses and is not engaging. They contain words like integrity, service, treat, respect, and others that do not address what the business owners expect from the people in the business.

The wording can be vague and does not convey the true meaning of the mission, vision, and values of the business.

What is your specific mission?

What value does your product or service provide to the customers, clients, employees, and to the world in general?

What is the purpose for your business?

What values do you hold to be true and are steadfast for your business?

Can others clearly understand what your business is all about?

In a business I owned, I had a mission, vision, and values but they were all in my head and never written down. I think I expected others in the business to know what the vision, mission, and values were by osmosis.

At least it seems that way if they are not clearly articulated to the employees, managers, and others. The clients knew that we had values based on our work ethics.

Do your customers or clients know what your business stands for?

What values you hold to be true?

Have clear statements for your business that are not vague but easily understandable by anyone who reads them.

If you don't, how can you be sure that everyone else knows what your business is about?

Every person ends up somewhere in life. Some end up where they are on purpose and not by chance or someone else's plan.

These people have a vision and a clearly defined purpose for their life and their business. They have a dream that they are following and striving toward. They want to accomplish something of value or they want to leave a legacy to the next generations. They have a calling on their life and a set of strategies to accomplish their goals and objectives.

Do you have a clear picture of where you want your business to be in the next 1, 3, 5 or more years?

Do you know what your business will look like when it is able to run without you? Will your business be able to run without you being present?

What would happen if you were not able to be present in your business?

Your business may be progressing along a certain track, but is it on the right track?

Is it reaching new heights?

You are able to keep an eye on the details (from a distance) and are confident that you are informed of the business status.

How does it feel to have this kind of business environment?

You could relax and enjoy your business. It is possible!

Successful business owners and managers have many things going for them. Among them, they have a vision and a purpose. They have the courage to take action on their vision.

They follow through on their action steps to reach their goals and objectives, which increase their chances for success. On the other hand, if they lack the vision and purpose it leads to disorganization, frustration, confusion, and mediocre results at best.

If you don't have a target that you are aiming for, you will hit it every time. But what good is that?

What is your target? Can you see it clearly?

Are you aiming in the right direction?

Do you know your destination?

Professional athletes are trained and skilled to make it look easy, but they spend hours in training and perfecting their skills that most people don't see.

Imagine a pro golfer not having a caddie that he or she can discuss the next shot with. Do you think they would perform as well? Imagine if the holes on the golf course moved every 5 minutes or less. Would the golfer be able to judge where the hole (target) is going to be?

Do you have moving targets in your business?

Many times highly trained and skilled business owners and managers are not achieving their highest potential because they do not have a clearly defined mission, vision, and values for their business.

Without a purpose and vision for the business to direct the day-to-day business decisions, they can get trapped in the urgent issues and spend most of their time IN the business and very little time ON the business,

You are just getting up to the tee and swinging away.

Without vision, the people will perish.

Just like the Titanic, they hit an iceberg and collapse in a sea of issues.

You spend time working the issues that squeak the loudest or most often. Therefore, the squeaky wheel gets the grease. You are far too busy putting out fires and greasing squeaky wheels to be more strategic about the plans for your business.

Helen Keller once said when asked, "What would be worse than being blind?"

She said, **"To have sight without vision."**

A business owner needs to have a business plan that is structured in such a way so that it addresses the vision and purpose for the business.

This plan is a strategic part that holds the business together, like the links that keep all of the train cars attached together.

Having a clearly defined plan and purpose in place allows you to effectively measure your progress toward your vision and to keep moving forward. When a train stays in the same place or goes in reverse it takes that much longer to get to their destination.

Is your business in status quo or a declining mode?

By evaluating your mission for your business and reflecting on where you see the business going into the future, you can have a clearer picture for what you want from and for the business. The benefits of having clarity in your business mission, vision, and values are worth their weight in gold.

You plan and determine your destination when you take a trip or a vacation, so why would you have a business without a plan and a destination. You make sure you have enough money to finish the trip. You make sure you have all the supplies you need, places to sleep, places to eat, and what sights to see.

No Plan and No Destination or KNOW PLAN and KNOW DESTINATION!

What about you? Do you have a plan for your business?

Is it clear to everyone in or outside of the business?

Do you have specific action steps to take daily to move your business along the path of the plan?

Are you building your business with the end in mind?

If so, what is your end in mind?

Do you have a plan for a successor for your business?

Do you have an option in mind or will you sell the business?

Will there be a value to the business without you?

There are so many questions that need to be addressed.

Some business owners and managers start with a clear vision in their mind, but along the passing of time they lose sight of their mission, vision, and values.

With all of the issues that are vying for their attention, they forget about their vision and why the business was started. Many times you end up with products or services that do not match the original intention of the business.

You don't know how you got to this place. Is this you? If so, you need to revisit your mission, vision, and values and determine what needs to change. You cannot change the past, but you can build a future.

Does your business support your life or is your business your life?

You started a business for a reason. Do you remember what it was? As my Dad wrote in a high school yearbook "You only get out of life, what you put into it."

You are feeling stagnant, mediocre, stuck in the responsibilities of running your business, and have lost your sense of fun and enjoyment with the business endeavor.

You need to create a vision and purpose for building your business into the future.

What does that look like to you?

Do you need to make some changes or reevaluate where you are heading?

What can a clear mission, vision, and values provide for you and your business?

Here are a few nuggets of what this can do for you and your business:

1. A mission, vision, and values statements that are clear and understandable energizes and excites you and your people. Many successful business owners and managers understand this. Their vision and purpose are heart felt and ingrained in their mind. It stirs up their thoughts and ignites them to reach for the desired outcome.

If they can't feel it, they can't see it! Therefore, if your vision and purpose doesn't motivate and inspire others, you may need to contemplate and revise it, so that it is absolutely clear as to what you really desire. If you can see it, then you can feel it. It is visible in all that your business does and is. It permeates the business environment.

2. A purpose that puts a fire in your belly.
You are emotionally tied to the outcome of your purpose and want to strive to see results. It helps you to overcome the daily distractions and obstacles that seem to get in the way. You can imagine what it will be like to see your business thriving and soaring above your competition. You are a human being, not just a human doing.

3. Your vision and purpose match with your values. You have a reason to get up in the morning. You can't wait to focus your efforts on reaching the objectives for the day that lead you closer to your vision. You value each and every person you come in contact with and realize that they are a human being, just like you.

You matter. They matter. You have a sense of meaning and feel good about what you do. You have a connection between your current state and your future. You are able to push through difficult situations and know they are only temporary setbacks.

Determine what you want and why you want or need it. Ask others to assist you in reaching your mission and vision, while adhering to your values.

What will happen if you don't create a mission, vision, and values for your business?

Will it change on its own?

I don't think so!

In order to soar above the crowd and reach new heights, you need to have a clear mission, vision, and values to move your business above and beyond your competition.

To Soaring above the Crowd!

Light at the End of the Tunnel

"A leader has the vision and conviction that a dream can be achieved. He inspires the power and energy to get it done." - **Ralph Lauren**

"A leader's role is to raise people's aspirations for what they can become and to release their energies so they will try to get there." - **David Gergen**

You are a leader.

Do you know who is following?

Is anyone following your lead?

If not, when you look behind you and no one is following, you may just be out for a walk.
Leaders are readers and readers are leaders.

What does it mean to be a leader?

It means that you are out front. You have to be able to see what is coming and take action so that your business keeps going in the right direction. You are able to see beyond what is right in front of you and also not neglect it. You may have developed tunnel vision and are unable to see the light at the end, which is your destination.

You do have a definite destination, right?

Your ability to lead by example determines the effectiveness of your business. If your leadership is an effective example and you are leading by serving others, your business will grow and prosper into the business of your dreams and aspirations. Your example can either increase or decrease the rate of growth of others in the business. The business is a direct reflection of your leadership as the owner or manager.

You need to be a leader developer not just a leader.

It does not matter the size of your business, you must be developing your leadership skills in order for the business to move forward and not remain status quo or mediocre at best. You are the one who sets the direction for the business.

You had many ideas for your business when you started or purchased the business. You may have lost sight of the business direction and you want to regain it. You are confident that others know what you see as the business vision. You still have the same vision, but have you shared it with your people? Are you able to articulate what you see as the mission for the business so that it is clearly understood by others? Do you customers or clients know why you are in business? How about your suppliers or vendors?

Many business owners create mission statements that they frame and post on the walls of their business. Many of these statements are rarely read or many times not even followed by the people in the business. Many of the statements I have seen lack clarity as to what they really mean. The wording is very similar to or the same as many other businesses. They contain words like integrity, service, treat, respect, and others that do not address what the business owners expect from the people in the business. The wording can be vague and does not convey the true meaning of the vision, mission, and values of the business.

Your company has a mission statement, but it is not intended to be motivational tool, but a management tool. The statement helps to guide all of the operations in a business. It should be used when interviewing new candidates for employment or even your suppliers. They are considered when making strategic business decisions. It is used in conjunction with your values. All of these statements are referenced when conducting periodic performance reviews. They help to determine whether someone is eligible for a pay raise and promotion. They define the specific reasons some employees may be terminated.

Your vision for the business clearly defines the "personality" of the business and the specific objectives or goals that your people are trying to attain. The vision and light you are striving toward are one of the most powerful accountability tools you can develop, if you do it right. Imagine all of your people always being on the same page and able to see your ideas come to light!

What is a *Vision Statement*: It is an explanation of why the business exists and what its purpose is. It states the long-term objectives and the overall governance and tone of the company. Think of it as a combination of a "Who we are," "Why we're here" and a "Where we're going" statement. A vision statement is "future oriented." It is your company's "Declaration." It needs to answer the WHY question.

To assist you in drafting your vision statement, you need to ask yourself the following questions and write down your honest answers:

• Why did you start (or buy or take over) the business?

• How and why is the business important to you, your people, your customers or clients, and your community?

• What does your company do? Why do you do it?

• Why makes your business special or different?

- Why should people want to work at your business?

- Why should your customers or clients buy from you instead of your competitor?

- What are your specific goals and objectives?

- Why are those goals and objectives important to you and your people?

- Any other questions you think are important in defining who your business is, why it exists, and what your company is going to accomplish.

As you answer the questions, please be "future oriented". Focus on the light at the end of the tunnel. Don't worry about where you are now relative to the questions. Instead, be specific on where you desire to be relative to the questions.

Don't try to create a masterpiece and don't try to feel like you have to impress anyone with it.
Be genuine in your words. Say what you mean.

Also don't get hung up on the length of your vision statement. It may only be two or three sentences; it might be a full-page long. The length doesn't matter, but the content does.

The vision statement must touch you emotionally. You can feel it personally and it has clarity and is concise. It is a statement you resonate with and can stand behind.

You want your people to be able to endorse and support it. It is not written in stone so you will need to be able to modify it, if needed. You need to get to the heart of what's truly important to you. If not, you need to keep answering the questions until it is very clear and gets to the heart of the matter.

You are taking one step at a time and the light is getting bigger and brighter. Celebrate how far you have come along the way and take time to reflect on your progress. You now have a vision and can truly see the light at the end of the tunnel. You have direction and a destination.

Keep chugging along and you will see the light at the end of the tunnel become clearer.

All Aboard

"I am convinced that nothing we do is more important than hiring and developing people. At the end of the day you bet on people, not on strategies." *- Lawrence Bossidy*

"Do not hire a man (or woman) who does your work for money, but him (or her) who does it for the love of it." *- Henry David Thoreau*

You have hired employees since starting your business and since then you have let some of them go.

You determined that you might not have had a clear picture of the person you hired for the position. You want to have a much better description for your expectations of the employee prior to the hiring process.

Create an on boarding process that clearly defines the type of person you are looking for.

Have job descriptions for each position in order for it to be clear.

Do you have specific requirements and testing to verify if the person can perform in the position?

Do you have a method for interviewing and narrowing down the applicants to the best possible fit for your business?

Is your business vision clear and do your employees GET it?

Do they Grasp, Engage, and Tackle it?

Grasp It: Employees are able to understand the business direction and why you are in business.

Engage in It: Employees take responsibility to help the business move in the direction. They come to work in the business in order for the business to grow and prosper.

Tackle It: Employees have the right skills to capitalize on them. They use their skills in a methodical and repeatable fashion regularly.

How do you know that the person will be a good or great employee?

It's not all about the person that you hire as much as it whether they resonate with the mission, vision, and values of your business. Do you have a clear mission, vision, and values for your business? Clear and concise statements about your business are shared with prospective employees during the interview process.

By being clear, your statements cannot be misinterpreted by a prospective employee. Find people who are driven, innovative, and energetic. You need to have all of your employees, managers, and others on the same page which means they are on board. All Aboard!

Empower your employees to take initiative in handling customer or client issues. Allow them to take some calculated risk and to be creative. They may have the very best solution to an issue.

Have a clear and concise job or position description and you interview only the people who are qualified for the job. Pre-qualify prospective employees using means other than a direct face-to-face meeting.

I have hired people based upon what they say in the interview process and later find out they could not perform as they said they could.

Many business owners have fallen prey to the same types of hiring issues. Not everyone can do what he or she claims they can do. You may be using statements that can be misunderstood.

Some businesses have a process for pre-qualifying employees such as having them email a resume as an attachment, have a 10-question survey, and other ideas. The survey questions vary depending on the business, but some relate to the person's values like from a list of movies which did you like the best and why?

They narrow done the applicants to no more than 10 candidates. The ten candidates are then interviewed by phone. The candidate list is narrow done to 3 people. Each of the finalists is then asked to take a DISC profile study. The profile helps in determining if the candidate has the behavioral style that most matches what the position entails.

For instance, we know that a good salesperson will score higher in the 'D' (dominant) and 'I' (influential) category. A technician will score higher in the 'S' (steadiness) and 'C' (conscientiousness) category. By skipping any of these steps, you may end up with the wrong employee for the position. There is no guarantee that following these steps will eliminate the risk of hiring the wrong person, but it sure helps to know what you are getting.

Besides you as the owner or manager, your employees can be your most valuable assets. Having the right employees in the right positions can move your business beyond where you can imagine.

Having the wrong employees or in the wrong position can break your company.

I have worked with people who were the wrong person for the position and it can be very frustrating. They were put in a position because they had been part of the business for many years.

The owners did not want to let them go as they felt that the person was part of their family. The owners actually may be providing a blessing to the employee. The employee may be a better fit for another business and you may be holding back their growth and career path.

The strength of your business, it's products and services, is dependent on the strength of your employees. Are they a good team or do you have too many that are focused on me, myself, and I?

You trust your employees to get the job done but they may be focused on their job and not its effect on the business as a whole. This is why it is critical to have the right people in the right position. Do you have the right people on the train so that they are all aboard or on board? This can be easier said than done.

You as the owner or manager have put a lot on the line with all your blood, sweat, and tears over the years. You have invested your time and talents in growing the business. You have worn many hats when you started the business so you know what it takes to grow your business.

You have performed many of the roles as needed to keep the business moving forward. After all, the business depended on you during the early stage. It all rested on your shoulders and it is at your own risk. As the business owner you are still the one with the most risk.

You have spent long hours with endless tasks and demands on your time in order to build your business. You don't want to take chances with the future of your business. You feel the pressure and the responsibility to your customers, clients, suppliers, and your employees. The business was started in order to have control of your own situation. You wanted to utilize your skills and see the results in your own business. You have endured through lean times and you like the feeling of exhilaration when the business soars.

You don't just let anyone into your house, so why would you let just anyone into your business? Be determined to find the right people for your open positions that you can trust to do the job and to work with your other employees.

Understand that you cannot run your business alone. You've tried to run your business without the help of others and found that you can only endure that for so long. You need other people to fulfill specific roles in or for your business.

In one of my businesses, we thought we were saving money by hiring employees that had just finished their training as a computer programmer. We were a small business and we did not have the staff to spend time training the individuals so many times we had to take steps to modify the systems prior to installation. We should have spent the time to educate them on the project needs and follow up on any questions that they had. We expected them to know more than they did.

Don't fall into this trap of trying to save money. You get what you pay for. You may have to pay more but you will have to manage less.

Most business owners and managers will hire for the positions that they care the least for first. They will hire last for the positions that they like, are capable in, or the most confident with. Do you have a difficult time delegating responsibility for that position?

Having always performed the work needed for the business you may have found that if you delegated tasks you could spend more time creating a vision for your business into the future. We do not know what the future holds, but we can prepare for it.

Do you spend a majority of your time IN the business? This is very common and I see it all the time!

You may lack a clear hiring process and be forced to deal with hiring when you urgently need another person for a position. An employee is fired or they leave voluntarily, then you scramble to fill the position.

Many feel the pressure of not having a replacement so they hire a friend, family member, someone who is unemployed, or someone who was recommended for the position. You may know someone at your church or other association is looking for a job so you decide to give him or her a try.

Would you try a doctor for surgery? Would you hire a friend with no experience to build your house?

When you decide to hire a person for a position in your business do your due diligence to find the best person you can for the position. When you hire family or friends you may be putting them and yourself in a tough position, if it does not work out. You know them prior to hiring them, so that can put your relationship at risk. I have made some of these missteps in hiring for my business.

I hired a friend who was unemployed with the thought that I was helping him out. I came to the realization that he was not the right person for the job. I was also unable to work with him regularly to keep him moving. I was spending most of my time with customers so I was rarely in the office.

I have consulted with family owned businesses and many have a difficult time firing a family member from the business. The family members can be the hardest to get to work for the business. They may think they deserve to work for the family business after all, they are a part of the family.
Do they really want to be part of the business or do they just want to receive a dividend?

Your business may be better served by paying them a dividend to stay out of the business. You could hire a person that could bring more experience or motivation to the position and that can help to move your business to the next stage.

Before hiring for a position here are some of the questions you might ask yourself:

- Is this position needed for our overall mission, vision, and values?

- Why are we hiring and what is the purpose of this position?

- Is the position clearly defined and necessary?

- Do we have a current employee who is the right person for this position?

- Are we just hiring to fill a position for someone who left or was fired?

- Is this a full time position or could we outsource it?

- Do we have a hiring system in place so that we know when we have the right person for the position?

Take the time to find the right person. Many business owners and managers do not spend the correct amount of time to secure the best employee for the job. Hiring can be a shot in the dark and then you hope it works out.

Do the following in order to have a clear hiring process or system:

- Prepare your ads or job posts so that you attract the right people

- Search on-line databases like LinkedIn for qualified candidates. You can also see where they worked previously or who they are connected with

- Search social networks to see what the candidates are talking about

- Take time to clearly define the position (you may want the person to do more for the business than a prior employee)

- Have a list of questions to ask candidates during an interview in order to prequalify them

- Have a clear picture of what you are offering them and do they fit your business culture.

Share your mission, vision, and values.

I have found that many business owners and managers hire based upon a need to fill a position without having a specific plan for how they would like to see the position evolve. You assume the person is going to handle the position just like you would.

You hire a salesperson and expect them to be out making sales calls every day. You think they are not doing their job because that is not how you would do it. You may have already had connections in order to make sales calls so you rarely had to call on new prospects. They have a sales background but it may not be the same clientele as your business.

It will take them some time to generate leads, prospects, customers, and clients. You may have an idea in your head about how many new customers or clients you need for your business. Have a written plan for how to get the new customers or clients. Have good marketing materials that are used consistently. Is your marketing hit or miss and inconsistent? You may have a perceived brand in your head but it is not consistent across all the mediums that are currently in use today. Have a specific call to action on each marketing effort.

Have consistent training and continuing education that is clearly defined. Encourage your employees to attend training and have a process for determining if they are retaining what they were taught. Do you provide reimbursement for continuing education?

Do you bring other businesses in to provide training for your employees? You may assume they have all the training that they need, as they were hired because they already had the prior education and training for the position.

Many businesses offer training that is inadequate or lacks clarity.

How do you know what they learned?

Do they apply what they learned or does it just get forgotten?

Knowledge and understanding are two different things. Knowledge + understanding = education. You need people who apply their education in your business to make it better.

Successful business owners and managers value training and have a process or system to evaluate the benefits of the training. When you hire a new employee you enable them to get a picture of what other people in the business do.

If you are a manufacturer, you allow your new employees to get a sense of the types of products you produce. You take them to the plant for a tour and allow them to ask questions about a particular area. They see that the position is bigger than just what they do. They need to see its effect on other employees, managers, and the owners.

Encourage your employees to join organizations that can help them to improve their leadership skills such as a rotary, a group, or association that matches their position, or Toastmasters.

I have been in Toastmasters for a number of years and I continue to attend regularly as I always learn something new. It has increased my communication and leadership skills beyond what I could have imagined.

When I joined Toastmasters I thought that it would be a short-term membership. I have since been a leader in my area and also have made many friends that I would not have otherwise. I have used the training from being a member also in order to make me a better speaker and presenter. I know it works!

Are you leaving training to chance?

You need to take it seriously. Be intentional in your hiring and training. It will benefit the business much more than you may think. I recall taking courses over the internet when I worked for a business.

The course prepared me to implement an electronic forms solution, which the business had not previously entertained. I was able to present the solution as a value to the business. This created a great time saver for the business!

Does everything in your business have all of the processes or systems in place so that a new employee can just hit the ground running?

The new employee actually had different processes and systems where they worked previously. They are not familiar with your processes and systems, so you need to spend some time training them on the use of yours. You believe that your processes are clear, which they may be to you. A new employee may bring some new ideas that may make your processes and systems more efficient than they already are.

Do you have periodic performance reviews at least yearly? Provide feedback to your employee that is valuable and encouraging to him or her.

Have a consistent method for evaluating your employee's performance. Do not neglect having periodic reviews, as you know that they are not directly tied to an increase in pay.

I have consulted with businesses that have failed to give at least an annual performance review because they thought that they would have to give the employee a raise. The employee asked for a review and was informed that it was not necessary as they were doing a good job. What does it mean, that they are doing a good job?

Your employees many times are not looking for an increase in pay, but they are looking for feedback on how they can improve in their position or career path. You may be holding them back since you are not providing feedback that includes actions that the employee can take to improve.

Provide meaningful feedback that encourages your employees to expand their skills. Address any issues that your employee reveals, that are having an effect on their performance.

Provide the tools and supplies for your employees to be able to work smarter not just harder. This can motivate your employees to look for ways to improve their function in the business.

They may also look for ways to improve the performance of others. Your employees are open to change and embrace it, as they know it is inevitable. Your employees take the initiative in finding solutions not just bringing up issues.

Salary is not the only way to compensate your employees. There are a number of different ways to provide a competitive compensation package like vacation time, profit sharing, retirement fund contributions, insurance (health and life), disability insurance, etc.

By having some of these additional options you also gain some employee loyalty. You are able to reward them beyond a pay increase for a job well done. Regularly praise your managers and employees for the job they are doing, even when you think they can do better. **It only takes a minute!**

All business owners that I have been in contact with agree that good employees are hard to find and keeping them can be difficult. It doesn't have to be this way. You need to treat your employees the way you treat your best customers or clients. By being a caring and encouraging business owner or manager you can build a winning team. Get them all on the same track and don't let your business be derailed by people problems.

Have a clear path to understanding and assessing employee engagement that starts with understanding employee experiences specifically, the critical touch points in the employee life cycle.

If you don't, here are five steps you can take to transform your employees' experiences and move the needle on engagement.

1. Make their job search simple, seamless, and informative.

Your prospective employees are forming opinions about your organization before they interact with you, which not only affects your recruiting efforts but also long-term engagement.

According to the Employee Experience Survey, up to 82 percent of your job prospects are still relying on your company website as a primary means for learning about your company, but of those that do, almost 40 percent feel the information isn't valuable.

What did we learn?

Ensure that your careers page and all public-facing job listings are current, informative and meaningful. They are also searching social media sites like LinkedIn to find people they may know that work for your business.

2. Create accurate first impressions.

Can a simple job interview have an impact on long-term engagement? Yes, definitely. Many applicants feel misled by the interview process and are less likely to be engaged as a result. Make sure that the position you are marketing during the hiring process reflects the role that the candidate will actually fill. Do you have clear position description? Do they fit with your business values?

3. Make the first day meaningful.

Many people describe their first day on the job as disorganized, dull, or confusing, which ultimately leads to lower levels of long-term engagement. Create a meaningful first day with an orientation experience that provides new employees with information specific to their job functions and connects them to the company's mission, vision, and values.

4. Give employees a structured onboarding experience.

Employee excitement wanes dramatically over the first three months of employment, and maybe that is to be expected. But we also know that most employers do not have any kind of structured onboarding approach during their first 90 days on the job. Therefore, employees are more likely to have lower engagement. Is this just a coincidence? Not likely.

5. Show them a path to success.

Employees want to know where their careers are headed, and having conversations about future options is incredibly important to retaining your most valuable people. This seems like a no-brainer, right? It may be, but most employees aren't having those conversations during the hiring process, and many aren't even having them during annual performance reviews. While many companies have established career-development programs, it's also beneficial to promote these programs and monitor them for effectiveness.

While employee engagement can be an elusive and subjective concept, we know that people who are invested in their jobs are more productive and have longer tenures than those who are not. For example, surveys have shown that a large percentage of U.S. employees reported overall satisfaction with their current job, but just over 1/3 of employees indicated that they were "very satisfied," while less than ½ reported that they were "somewhat satisfied."

Your business needs to take an active role in increasing overall employee satisfaction, and you can do so by turning the key moments in the employee life cycle into a meaningful journey.

Remember that your employees can make or break your business. They are your greatest assets. **Learn how to hire right so that you have to fire less!** It is much better in the long run to get the right people on the train and going in the right direction.

All Aboard!

On the Right Track

"If I had nine hours to chop down a tree, I would spend the first six sharpening my axe." *- Abraham Lincoln*

"Always focus on the front windshield and not the review mirror." *- Colin Powell*

Many business owners and managers often overlook the idea of strategic planning.

They say that it is unnecessary and that they know what they are doing without it. They just don't have the time to spend ON their business because they are spending most of their time IN the business.

This can get you off track quickly. You don't have a specific plan to reach your goals. You may not have written goals but you have goals in your head.

Your goals are vague or non-existent if you are the only one who knows what they are. Do you have a big goal for your business or personal life? You may not believe that you need to create goals.

I know that I have fallen into this trap myself. We tend to think that we will get to something when we have the time. If you are like me the time never seems to be available. I recall reading a book called "If You Don't Have Time to do It Right, When will You Have Time to do It Over?"

You are NOT alone. Many if not most business owners have a difficult time creating goals that are strategic for their business and personal life. You may have heard of having a BHAG, which is a Big Hairy Audacious Goal. It is a goal that is bigger than anything you think you can do. It helps you to focus on a bigger picture and what can be possible. Do you have a BHAG?

Your goals and objectives for your business need to match your vision, mission, and values for your business. Your business is a reflection of you.

The direction of your business is dependent on your ability to clearly articulate your destination.

Is your business on the right track?

What are some ways that you can keep your business on the right track? As a business owner or manager do you know what your financial statements are telling you? You review these statements at least monthly and understand what they mean.

You track your cash flow, your expenses, and your liabilities in order to make clearly informed decisions that help keep your business on the right track.

Financial statements are good tools for running a business, but many times they only address what has already taken place. In order to address this shortcoming, you need to develop a scorecard that can be reviewed more frequently.

This scorecard can include key performance indicators (KPIs), percentages, ratios, and other information that will give you insight on a regular basis like weekly or daily. What is the information that you can use to do this?

Some examples might be:
- Productivity of employees
- % of marketing to sales generated
- Quotes won or lost
- % of sales expense to sales generated
- average A/R collection days
- average A/P days paid
- lead times

There are numerous examples that relate to specific industries. What do other businesses in your industry use to track as a scorecard or KPIs? Your industry associations may have some good ideas. Do you have employees that worked for a competitor? They may have some good input.

Do You Have a Caboose?

"I am convinced that nothing we do is more important than hiring and developing people. At the end of the day you bet on people, not on strategies." *– Lawrence Bossidy*

"Do not hire a man (or woman) who does your work for money, but him (or her) who does it for the love of it."
– Henry David Thoreau

Do you have people in your business who are just along for the ride? Do they only work for your business in order to collect a paycheck? Do you have people who are always finding something wrong and not suggesting solutions to the issues?

Are you constantly putting out fires that are caused by others who do not have the same vision for the business? Do people who constantly ask you to intervene or to come up with the solution to their problem stress you? You know that there has to be a better way. Let me assure you that you are NOT alone.

Remember when you started your business? Everyone on your team wore different hats because you could not afford to hire specialists or the more experienced people.

You all worked hard and got it done. You all put your hearts and souls into making the business succeed. Everyone thought of it as "their" company, even though most didn't have any shares of company stock.

They all pitched in and got on the train. Everyone got the train moving together in the same direction.

The furnishings left something to be desired. The office space was cramped and smelled bad. Your office equipment was constantly failing. Your website was always "under construction" for many months!

Remember when it was payday? You started the day asking "Who really needs their check today and who can wait until next week?" "Do you really need your expense check, or can it wait a few more days?"

Even though the pay was a little low and the hours were long, everyone had passion in his or her work and in seeing the business grow. You worked in unison toward a common goal. The bonds of friendship and camaraderie were solid. You were all doing battle together! Those truly were the "good old days."

Years may have passed and your business has changed direction gradually. You have hired additional people who may not share the same values that you originally intended for your business. Your start-up team is still there, but they are now in higher-level positions.

None of your employees are required to work excessive overtime anymore. Everyone is paid much more than in the early days. The benefits are better; there's more vacation time and more benefits. The company's survival is no longer threatened, as it was in your first couple years in business.

But things just don't feel the same. As you've added new employees over the years, the once dynamic "Whatever It Takes" culture has faded. Your old "war dogs" that sweated with you in the early days have lost their fire. The new cadre of employees just doesn't understand that their "job description" includes anything and everything they can do to serve your clients better. The tightness of your team has been replaced with cliques, gossiping, and backstabbing.

You've held periodic staff meetings, but they have not been real effective. You've begged and encouraged your leaders to help you get things back on track. You even had a company picnic. The business isn't much of a picnic anymore. Nothing seems to work.

Face it, even you have been affected or infected. You used to do twice as much work in half the time. You used to have goals, fueled with vision and passion. There was a fire in your belly. But now, you've settled for mediocrity and the status quo.

You have a gnawing feeling in your gut, though. The business culture isn't what it should be and you "wish" things could be different. You wish you and your team had that passion again. You wish your work had the meaning it once did. You don't know what to do to get it back and you're not even sure you have the energy to try any more.

Jack Welch (former Chairman of General Electric) said, "You pay a person for his or her hands, but they'll give you their brains and their hearts for free. All you have to do is ask!"

When's the last time you asked your team and your employees for their opinions? How they feel about the current business culture? What they love about their work or hate about it? What they would change about your company if they had the power to do it? What are their goals and aspirations? What are your goals and aspirations? Do they know what your goals are?

Do they realize how other employees are dragging down the business? Does anyone know what it is costing your business in profits, profit margin, customers, repeat business, supplier relations, and employee retention?

What does your team think about their current compensation plans? What's more important to them; increased health benefits, more time off, dress-down days, free lunches once in a while or increased pay? Do they know what needs to be accomplished in order for them to realize these added benefits?

People shouldn't be rewarded simply for showing up. They should be compensated according to the individual results each person brings to the company.

When pay-raises are distributed equally, the stronger players on your team will rightfully be frustrated that their individual, exceptional results are not being acknowledged.

Likewise, you're robbing your weaker players of incentive to become better. Think back to high-school sports; How would you have felt if you practiced hard and sacrificed in order to be a better player, but the coach decided that everyone gets to play the same amount of time regardless if they attended practice or not? Would this motivate you to want to play hard? Of course not! So don't do this now. Don't give pay-raises equally. Reward the best people with the highest raises or bonuses.

Here's another simple truth that we sometimes overlook: *People are not entitled to receive a pay raise each year.* Yes, you want to reward and retain your great people who bring you the best results and annual pay raises are one way to accomplish that. But the flipping of pages on a calendar does not signify an obligation to give a pay raise to everyone. The point is; pay raises and bonuses should never just be *given*. They should be *earned*.

Why are there cliques? Does your team trust you? Do they trust the other managers? Do they think of their current employment as a career, or just a job until something better comes along?

Remember, every dollar that you reduce in overhead directly impacts your company's bottom line: profits. "Labor" often accounts for an overwhelmingly significant portion of your overhead. If you can reduce that by even one percentage point, how much additional profit would you realize?

It will take time, effort, and attention to every detail. You'll have to make some gut calls and maybe even make unpopular decisions. But the return on investment could be substantial.

Who is in the caboose, just along for the ride?

Who is Feeding the Engine?

"If you live each day as if it were your last, someday you'll most certainly be right." *Steve Jobs*

"Life is a journey, not a destination." *Ralph Waldo Emerson*

What values are feeding your business? Is it the right fuel for your business engine? Does it burn efficiently and give the business the power to thrive not just survive. Do you have the right mixture of fuel or people to keep your business on track? As the business owner or manager you know what to feed the business engine. You are constantly reviewing the efficiency of the business and how you can make it more efficient. You're not just using the same fuel that you have always used, but are evaluating it regularly.

Your people are in the right positions and have the right processes to monitor the business when you are unable to be present.

They know what to look for and how to implement plans in order to build in more efficiency. They know the standards for how the business needs to be run. They have benchmarks and studies that they can rely on.

Even when you are unable to be present you have systems and processes in place that you can monitor from a distance. You are confident that the information produced by your systems and processes is accurate and current. They reflect what is truly happening in the business. You periodically review the accuracy of the information and don't assume that nothing has changed.

You have methods for generating qualified leads and referrals for your business. These methods have been developed over the years and they continue to show results. If the results are inadequate or lackluster, you seek to find out why. In order to improve the results you search for answers that can help you to increase quality leads. Keep a pulse on what your competition is doing and know what is being said about your business in the marketplace. Do you consistently monitor the status of your business and personal reputation in your area?

You have a process for keeping in touch with your prospects and customers or clients that is on going and not "hit or miss". Consistently keep your products and services in front of them. Send them articles or information that may be beneficial to them. Help them to not let you fall out of their sight; otherwise you become what I call "out of sight, out of mind".

Your methods for generating leads are consistent and replicable. All of your people realize that they are all in sales even though they are not in the sales department. Every contact with a prospect or customer or client has an effect on your business. It can be a bad experience with any employee that can be detrimental to your business.

Train all of your employees to be courteous to your customers, clients, and suppliers. You understand that bad news travels much faster than good news.

The people who have a bad experience share it with 7 times as many as those who have a good experience.

When it comes to lead generation, there is one thing that we can agree on: High quality leads are important. Here are some great tips to improve your lead generation process.

1. Identify Your Potential Buyer Knowing your ideal prospect's characteristics is important for lead generation. This discovery process should also involve sales, because it's critical to successful lead generation to align with sales about the ideal characteristics and when a lead should be passed to sales people.

2. Understand Them More than just identifying their demographics, you also need to understand their particular nuances. Know what motivates them, what their pain points are, how they like to receive communications, and where they get their information. Formalizing all this into a persona you can target is a great way to standardize all your lead generation processes.

3. Create a Marketing Database and Keep it as Accurate as Possible Have a formal process in place for staying on top of your data for lead generation. Realize that it is important to take the time to understand the current state of your company's database, how much better it could be, and the cost to get there. What is it costing you when it isn't accurate?

4. Understand their journey and Map Content Accordingly Regularly talk to your customers or clients about their buying process. Understand their journey and how they prefer to receive information, map out the journey, match it to the assets you have. You then identify where the gaps are in your content.

5. Create Relevant Content Send the right content to the right people in the way that they want to receive it and know that it is critical to your success. There is a lot of content that exists in the world today, but most of it isn't going to have meaning for your target. As a result, it's essential to differentiate your business as a solution provider that knows what they want. Providing relevant content proves that point, so it is critical.

Sometimes moving away from old lead generation strategies can be challenging. It's important to continue to evaluate your strategy to determine what is working, what is not, what needs to be fixed, and what is confusing about it.

The buying process is always changing, so you need to find new ways to reach your ideal prospects and to be heard through the noise. Instead of finding customers with mass advertising and email blasts, you must now focus on being found and learn to build continuous relationships. What makes your business different?

The days of relying solely on outbound marketing such as tradeshows, cold calls, and print ads for lead generation are over.

Your ideal prospects are taking more control of the buying process by educating themselves on your product and services and also your competitors. This happens long before your sales people ever reach them. Your job is not only to find leads, but it is to help leads find you. That is called Inbound Marketing.

Use inbound marketing and create interesting, informative, valuable, educational, and even entertaining content, and then optimizing and distributing it across different online mediums so that it can be found by and engage prospects early in their process.

As outbound marketing becomes less effective and more intrusive, inbound marketing takes on a bigger role in your marketing mix as defined in your lead generation plan.

Prospects have become overwhelmed with the wealth of advertising and they are getting much better at ignoring the messages they don't want to hear and researching what they do want to learn about. They are doing much more educating themselves before they look for a solution to their issue. Therefore, businesses must make sure that they build their digital presence as part of a lead generation plan.

Have strategies to develop demand for your products and services by educating your potential prospects about your offerings and the benefits.

Present your business in such a way as to get them to say to themselves that they want or need what your business provides. Be able to articulate why your business is different. You know why you are in business and it is reflected in your brand. Your brand is consistent throughout all of your communications.

Realize that not every prospect you identify will not be at the exact same stage along the sales pipeline. That is why you have a process of lead qualification that proves to be so vital, as it identifies the exact place in the process that a lead has reached and sends the offer needed to urge him or her closer to a purchase.

By automating this process you will take the manual labor out of it. Be open to systemizing your sales process in order for it to be more efficient and effective.

By having the ability to track your lead conversion rate, which is the number of leads it takes to gain a customer or client, you are able to plan better. How many leads are converted into customers or clients in a month?

There can be a dramatic impact in your bottom line by changing your conversion rate by just a percentage point. Determine the average selling price of your products and services so that you can evaluate what may happen if you increase the price. Changing either of these can have a very dramatic effect on your business profits!

Marketing and sales must be connected to the same overall objective, which is to secure new customers or clients. Marketing and sales alignment is a process, or the result of a process, that creates a mutual understanding and a partnership. Marketing and sales are able to share information without actually being present at a given location and they do it seamlessly.

You have a consistent flow in your sales funnel by having many avenues for people to find out about your business. Differentiate your business and promote it to the right audience.

Use all of your prospecting methods to keep your pipeline full. You routinely turn away business that is not a good fit for you.

Openly refer people that are not a good fit for your business to other businesses that would be. Not everyone is your target customer or client.

You know what they are looking for and you can articulate that to your referral partners. It is in giving that you receive.

Create a strategic network of people who are able to refer business to each other. They are competent people and businesses that you trust will provide a quality product or service. Your businesses complement one another and you have similar clients or customers. For instance, your businesses each serve business-to-business customers or clients or business-to-consumer.

Have a referral system that rewards those who consistently provide referrals and the referrals turn into qualified customers or clients. It is much easier to secure a referred prospect than someone who has no connection at all.

Value the person who referred the business and you want them to know how much you appreciate their efforts.

Encourage them by providing pre-qualified referrals to them as often as you are able. They are putting their trust in your business and they need to know the outcome.

Connect with them regularly in order to keep them informed of your progress. Ask them how you can refer more people to their business and how to know who they are looking for. What will a person say that would be a good referral?

How and what are you feeding your business engine?

Compartmentalized

"Success seems to be connected to action. Successful people keep moving. They make mistakes, but they don't quit." *– Conrad Hilton*

"The strength of the team is each individual member. The strength of each member is the team." *- Phil Jackson*

You are a business owner or manager who has many departments and functions that are performed within those departments in order for your business to run smoothly. You have come to depend on the services of the various departments and are comfortable with the results.

Are you ecstatic with the results or could they be even better?

Your people have become so departmentalized that they may not be communicating effectively with each other.

We could say they have become compartmentalized.

They only work on what is in their department function. They may not have an understanding of how their function or position interrelates with other functions in the business.

A good example of this would be an Information Technology person who decides what is best for the other people in the business by making decisions from his or her office and never interacting with the users of the systems.

Do you have people who don't get out in the business environment to see what is actually happening in other departments? Do you cross train your employees so they know what another person's position entails?

When people stay in their compartment and don't reach out to others, do you have a plan to help them to get out there and connect with others in the business?

You spend time as the owners interacting with your executive team. How about employees? Do they see you and run the other way? Do you provide positive comments and encouragement on a regular basis or do you only catch them doing something wrong?

Ask your executive team how their area or compartment is doing. Do they always say everything is fine because they don't want to tell you the truth? There is room for improvement in every business as it is the biggest room by far. You consistently encourage your executive team to look for improvements and you allow them to make suggestions. They will not lead the company astray. Trust their judgment and don't try to micromanage them.

Have clarity in your business and ensure that everyone knows your door is always open for him or her to share his or her observations and suggestions.

Take constructive criticism and don't get defensive. Be able to help them discover solutions on their own.

When a situation needs attention, coach them on how to resolve it. Don't allow people to bring their problems and issues to you and drop them at your doorstep. Be able to get the monkey off your back as they say.

Don't let others pass their monkey to you.

In order for your business not to become compartmentalized; lead by example. Develop leaders so that you are not the only leader. Be seen as a good example for others to follow.

If you think you are leading and you look behind you and no one is following, you may just be out for a walk.

Meet regularly with different areas of your business to understand their issues and to help them to resolve them. Consistently reach out to others in the business and do not play favorites.

I have been in many businesses that you can tell who the favorites are because other employees point it out.

They may not think the other person deserves to be given special treatment. They may be jealous or think it should be them.

They may believe that the person is just a YES person to everything the owner wants.

Having all YES people can be fatal to your business.

Is your business compartmentalized?

At Your Service

"A business absolutely devoted to service will have only one worry about profits. They will be embarrassingly large." *- Henry Ford*

"Spend a lot of time talking to customers face to face. You'd be amazed how many companies don't listen to their customers." *- Ross Perot*

Let's consider that your business is like a commuter train. You expect the train to arrive on time, get you to your destination on time, and to be comfortable and relaxing. You are able to rest and not worry about the ride or about being in control. You sit back and enjoy the ride.

Do you enjoy your business? How do your conduct your business?

You expect great service from the train business. Your expectations are not unreasonable. You are ecstatic if the train provides services that are beyond your expectations. You tell others about your experience.

What about your business, do you exceed your customers or clients expectations?

Your business provides excellent customer or client service. What is extraordinary customer or client service that makes it different? Most businesses claim to have good customer service. In order to have "extraordinary" customer service you need to go the extra mile and do what other businesses are not doing.

Many businesses view customer or client service as a department or area of their business that is handled by customer service representatives. It is not a department of your business; it is a mindset that permeates the entire business. Every person in your business affects your customer or client service. As I have called on some businesses, people who are less than enthusiastic about their job have greeted me. I felt like I was an interruption.

How do you serve your customers, clients, and even your suppliers?

Why would suppliers be included in customer service? You want your suppliers to treat you as you do your customers or clients. If you treat your suppliers as well as you do you customers or clients they will be more receptive to your needs. You want them to provide their products and services on time and within your budget, but how well are you working with them?

Periodically meet with your suppliers to discuss how you can work better together. Is it mostly a one-sided conversation, which is a monologue, not a dialogue? You tell them what you need and don't listen to what they need from you. You send them a purchase order and expect them to deliver on your terms.

You audit their business to determine if they are qualified to be a preferred supplier. You want to make sure they provide the best service for your business. Work more closely with them to benefit both of your businesses.

In growing your business it is beneficial to have competent suppliers so that you can deliver what you promise to your customers or clients.

Create a "WOW" experience with your customers, clients, and suppliers. Growing your business also includes having customers or clients that are in your specific target market.

Do you say YES to customers who are not the best fit for your business? If you do, your service will suffer.

It is truly amazing how the little things you do can have a big impact on your customers, clients, and suppliers. They make you stand out and **soar above the crowd!**

When I owned a previous business, I would give clients gifts at different times of the year. I recall finding pumpkins at a farmers market that were hand painted. I would purchase the pumpkins and hand-deliver them to clients. The pumpkins would have a tag with my business card attached. The pumpkin would be placed on the top of the receptionist's desk so that everyone in the business would see it along with his or her customers or clients.

Another example of extraordinary customer service is when I went on vacation to the east coast of the USA. I found a seafood store that sold fresh live lobsters. The store boxed up the lobsters in dry ice and I returned home with them. The next day I called some customers and delivered the fresh lobsters to the president's office. I proceeded to ask him or her to open the box. What an experience to see the look on his or her face when they opened the box. The lobsters were moving, much to their surprise and excitement. **What a thrill!**

Many business owners and managers do not provide the extraordinary customer or client service that they are more than capable of providing. All of the success in business is directly related to the little things that you do differently. It isn't mundane or by chance but it is by design.

I was at an advance professional business coach training session when the trainer sent out for a plaque to be created by a local printing business. The plaque was delivered the same day along with a bag of cookies. It is the little touches that leave a huge impression.

Give great attention to how your business serves your customers or clients and you will see repeat business as a result. Your customers or clients will speak highly of your business and tell others about why they work with you. You will spend less time marketing to find new customers or clients as you have a consistent referral base. Be constantly looking for ways to add value for your customers or clients. Be looking out for your customers' or client's best interests.

In my own businesses I have always looked for ways to help my clients by listening for what other products or services I could provide. When I completed a service call or implemented a product, I would ask if there was anything else they needed. Many times they would tell me something that they were thinking of doing.

If I knew someone that could help them I would setup a meeting with the other business and myself. We would collaborate on how we could work together for a solution. There are also times that I would step out of the way and let the businesses work together. My client would be getting their needs satisfied and they would still remain a client of my business.

I would look for ways to add value for my clients by asking if they had any plans in a certain area of their business such as bar code labels, electronic forms, new equipment, or specialized systems. They may say that they had not given it much thought. I would be able to present them with a particular solution and how it would help their business. This resulted in helping them to move forward and it benefited their business and mine.

Your customers or clients are the best source for your business to find out what inspires them and the direction of their business.

Focus on their needs and not your own agenda.

Also take to heart their feedback whether it is a criticism or an encouragement.

Periodically ask them how you are doing in providing products and services for their benefit. It doesn't matter the method you use to connect with them in a survey, but that you actually do it.

Find out what your customers or clients are saying or not saying to you about your business. Search the Internet for information that others are sharing about your business. Create alerts that can be emailed to you on a periodic basis. The alerts can be set up in reference to your business name, type of business, or other keywords.

Have methods for staying in contact with your customers or clients on a regular basis. Have a system or process for tracking when or how often you connect with them. Follow up with your customers or clients after the purchase.

Develop a company newsletter and send it out on a regular predetermined time frame. Connect with customers or clients about significant events in their business and personal life, if appropriate. Care more about them than just their business transactions with you. This increases your **Know, Like, Trust (KLT)** value with them.

Send your customers, clients, or prospects articles you think they may find interesting or that references their business or a similar business. Periodically contact them if they have not placed an order recently. If they decide to discontinue purchasing from your business, contact them to find out what caused them to do so. Remember to still keep in contact with them. You do not want to burn bridges!

I worked for a client on a part time basis for a few months until they hired a permanent person for a position. They had also offered me the permanent position, which I declined as I enjoy running my own business. A couple of years later the client contacted me to return for a full time contract for 3-6 months. I continued on the contract for over 8 months. They decided to hire a full time person for the position. I know they will contact my business when they have a need again.

I also have worked with businesses that have decided to find a person for less cost per hour. They worked with the other business for about a year. I contacted them to see how it was working out.

They asked if I could return to working for their business starting the very next day. That was over 30 years ago. They remain a client.

If you don't connect with your customers or clients regularly they tend to forget about all the products and services your business provides for them.

I have found times where they forget because my business was **"out of sight, out of mind"**.
Many businesses get tied up in their own day-to-day issues so they are not thinking about what you can do for them. They want to hear from you and know that they are important to your business.

If you don't, someone else will.

Many businesses do not have the loyalty to others, like it was a number of years ago.

You will experience, like I have, that if ownership or management changes there is a good likelihood that the new owners or managers will be looking for your replacement.

They many times have their own valuable connections, which they bring with them. I have seen businesses fail because some valuable people in the business leave and take customers and clients with them.

Be prepared!

Keep your customers or clients engaged so that they remember your business when they have a need.

Inform them when you have new products or services that may be of interest to them. Congratulate them when they get a promotion or are mentioned in a publication you read. Think about them when you want to meet someone for breakfast, lunch, or dinner. Periodically send them an email or some other form of communication to find out how they are doing. Send a personal note that encourages them or gives them hope.

You believe in under promising and over delivering, not the other way around. I think this saying is over used, but I know that many businesses have lost this concept.

Many businesses promise more than they can deliver. They give a prospect a lower price just to get in the door. Once the prospect becomes a customer or client then they steadily raise their prices. You may have had this happen to you, right? You decide that you will think twice before purchasing from them again.

Have processes and systems that help you to keep your promises and exceed your customer or client's expectations. Your customers or clients appreciate you going the extra mile to meet and actually exceed what they expect.

You always under promise and over deliver!

Don't make a serious mistake and leave customer or client service to chance. Have a set of questions to handle customer or client complaints. Come to a resolution as quickly as possible.

Have scripts that deal with some of the following issues that may occur:

- They are looking for a product or service that you don't provide

- They contact you when you are currently up to your eyeballs in work

- They ask questions that you need to get more information on

- They want to connect with someone else in your business

- They need technical assistance and you need to connect them to the right person

- They just want someone to talk to about another frustration unrelated to your business

- Who knows what? Be prepared to help them

What will you say to them? Be able to help them or direct them to someone who can. By preparing prior to the conversation, you are more in control of what your people will say.

Having scripts is just the beginning, as you will need to train your staff on using them. Without scripts or some form of response your staff is likely to make up their own, many times on the fly. Many businesses have numerous people that interact with their customers or clients. Therefore, why leave it to chance. Be intentional and proactive in how you handle customer interactions.

Your people are responsible and you can trust them in positions where they have consistent customer or client connections. Hire the right people for these positions so that your business is seen in a positive light. Interview and hire the people that best fit the mission, vision, and values for your business. They are friendly and cooperative in helping the customer or client. They answer the customer or client with a smile on their face. They enjoy coming to work for your business and display it in their daily attitude. Be confident that they are the right person for the job.

Your people know how to handle a dissatisfied customer or client. Have them trained on how to respond. Make sure they are able to use the opportunity to build loyalty and trust in your business. Are you confident and know you can trust them to follow up with the customer or client to resolve the issue?

You staff is trained on how to handle complaints by:

• Letting your customer or client know that the issue will be resolved.

• Actively listening to the customer's complaint and acknowledging it.

• Not being defensive or arguing with the customer.

• Restating the complaint in your own words so that the customer knows you understand the situation. Ask questions to clarify the issue.

• Giving the customer a sincere apology for the issue. Show the customer that you care. Some may not accept the apology, but give it anyway.

- Provide a solution to the issue even if you have to refund their purchase. You may be able to offer a replacement or a comparable product or service. You can also have them provide a written complaint so that you can present it to others in the business for response and training. You ask them how you can serve them better in the future.

Use every complaint as an opportunity to make your business better and to alleviate having the same issue in the future.

Ask your satisfied customers or clients if they would be willing to provide a testimonial or case study as to how you have helped their business to succeed or how they benefit from your products or services.

You post the testimonials and case studies on your marketing materials, your website, social networks, or other customer facing initiatives. Ask them if you can write a story on how you have helped their business and whether they would be willing to endorse it. Remember to share the story with them prior to publishing it. Post case studies on your website and as press releases or articles for your newsletter.

Your business is easy to do business with (ETDBW) and you welcome your customer or client's comments. Periodically survey your customers or clients using an outside service or a secret shopper. You may use a secret shopper to reveal how your competition is doing.

Use an outside person or service to make calls to your business at different times of the day to determine how effective your customer or client interface is. This can reveal issues within your business. You may be surprised at what you find.

Go ahead and provide Extraordinary Customer or Client Service!

Bridge Out

"If you can dream it, then you can achieve it. You will get all you want in life if you help enough other people get what they want. " - *Zig Ziglar*

"Take advantage of every opportunity to practice your communication skills so that when important occasions arise, you will have the gift, the style, the sharpness, the clarity, and the emotions to affect other people." – *Peter Drucker*

Your business is heading in the right direction. You are looking forward to the next stage of your business.

Your business is moving full steam ahead and you have the right people in place.

Your systems and processes are in place and working together. Your strategies and plans for all of your departments are in place and they work well together.

You have repeat business and are always looking for new products and services you can provide. Have a consistent lead and referral generation system. You can see the light at the end of the tunnel and are striving to reach your destination.

All of the sudden there is a roadblock in your plans.

There is a bridge out up ahead.

You don't know what happened to the bridge or how long it will take to fix it. If you continue in the same direction your business will go off a cliff or be derailed.

You have to either wait for the roadblock to clear (bridge to be fixed) or you have to back up and switch to a new track or direction. You could build a new bridge. Which will you choose?

You may decide to wait for the issue (roadblock to be removed) to be corrected so that you can proceed. How long are you willing to wait?

You contemplate the risks for your actions. You need more information before you decide what you will do.

You are unable to get more information, as no one knows how long it will be. You may struggle to make the right decision. You feel like your hands are tied. **You are NOT alone**. This happens to most business owners and managers at some point.

You may decide to backup and change direction. Will this take longer than waiting for the roadblock to clear? Is changing direction the right thing to do? Is the route you are taking still viable?

Will changing direction have an adverse effect on employees, customers or clients, and suppliers? Will changing direction not be in agreement with your mission, vision, and values?

Maybe it is not such a great idea. You may feel at times that you just don't know what to do in a particular instance.

There is no question that a steady amount of sales of new business is critical to the growth of your business.

If you totally neglect new sales your business could be set up for a disaster, which could be your roadblock. Do you have repeat customers or clients that you depend on for most of your sales?

I can relate to this issue as I depended on on-going work from my IT consulting business clients and when some of it dried up I had to scramble to find more business accounts.

Is all your business revenue on one track or do you have multiple streams (tracks) of income?

Don't wait for your customers or clients to go to a competitor. Be prepared for the worst and plan for the best.

What effect would this decision have on your bottom line of your business? Will it cause your business to struggle financially depending on your decision?

Will it mean having to find new customers or clients? Will you have to relocate the business?

Will it have an effect on employee morale?

So many questions and not enough time!

Can you be sure that you are making the right decision?

You have consulted with other advisors to help you get a clear picture of the situation. Have other business owners and managers encountered this roadblock? What did they do to overcome it?

Did they change direction or did they wait it out? Have you experienced this roadblock in the past? Is this a bridge you need to cross in order for your business to survive or thrive?

What are the ramifications of doing nothing?

Your staff and outside experts are giving you a clear picture of where the business is heading. They may not be focusing on the future or see the roadblock coming because they only have information for what has already happened as in the case of financial information.

Your financial information is mostly a snapshot of what has already occurred. Who owes you, who you owe, and how much you have accumulated.

You know that your business could do more and need to develop the functionality to look into the future. You must develop some projections into the future.

Some financial goals may not be visible to others but may be in your head. You have a gut feel for the business but it may not be the real facts.

As a business owner myself, I can remember running a business where I spent a majority of my time in the business.

I spent little, if any time planning for the future. By focusing most of my time in the business, the marketing to new clients was lacking. I was keeping an eye on the details more than creating a vision for the business.

Can you relate to this issue, the lack of forward thinking?

Can you honestly say to yourself that it is better to do nothing than to take a risk?

Is it truly a risk or will your business be better off by changing direction.

I have seen many business owners who have continued to sell the same products and services for years. They eventually go out of business because they did not change with the times. They provided products and services that kept declining in sales. They wanted to believe that there would always be a need for their products and services. They were not keeping an eye on their competition and the industry as a whole. The need for their products and services eventually became obsolete. This has happened numerous times in the technology industry, as it can change very quickly.

In order to be successful in business you **MUST** focus on the entire business, not just the areas you feel the most comfortable with.

Are you focused on your technical skills and not how to lead the business?

Are you focused on customer or client service but lacking in marketing your business?

Sales and marketing are not the same.

Maybe you're focused on hiring additional staff and not on reducing costs in other areas. Just adding people is not always the best option for a business.

Are you hiring the right people for the right position? Do you have the right people on the train? Are they all on the same track or the right track?

Is the industry that your business is in volatile to change at the drop of a hat or someone throwing a switch?

You know your business better than anyone else since you are the owner. You have been in this business for a number of years and are confident you are keeping up on the changes in the industry. Suddenly you face a decision that you thought you would never have to make.

Are you feeling like you are being forced into this decision because so much of it is beyond your control? Where do you turn?

A certified business advisor/coach can help you to evaluate the options that you have or may not have thought of.

What would it hurt to have another set of eyes to see the situation from a different perspective?

Business owners who "know it all" and don't think they need anybody to assist them, often fail in business, because they don't see the bridge out up ahead.

Even the most successful business owners and managers need to be willing to add to their business skills and to improve their vision.

In this age of ever changing technology, strategies, and tactics for business there will always be markets being discovered or discontinued. Are you going full steam ahead with no regard to the situations ahead of your business?

Just look at your post office and the reduction in direct mail and letters. Look at businesses that sell pre-printed forms or fax machines.

Do you know another business owner that was derailed by not keeping ahead of the times and was buried in their business? I have seen many businesses just decide to call it quits when they hit a roadblock.

Sometimes you are so busy with the operation of the business that you don't see what is coming your way. Everything is rolling along fine and you can't see it stopping anytime soon.

Are you paying attention to the signs?

Bridge Out Ahead!

It is like the old saying that we can't see the forest for the trees!

All Systems Go

"Everything must be made as simple as possible. But not simpler." - **Albert Einstein**

"System fails when people with ability don't have authority and people with authority don't have ability." - **Amit Kalantri**

What does it mean to have all systems and process working together in unison?

How efficiently would a train run if the wheels did not turn or the engine needed constant repairs?

All of the parts of the train have to be functioning correctly in order for the train to move forward. The train needs the right fuel, be on the right track, and be heading in the right direction.

We have processes and systems even in our personal life, like diets and exercise, so why not in our business?

If you have multiple people in your business that are doing the same job but each person is doing it differently, then only one person (at the most) is doing it the best way.

Everyone else is doing it in a less efficient and productive manner.

Without specific systems and processes that interrelate your business can have people running in circles. Many times businesses have several people looking for the same information.

Instead of finding out if someone already has the information they need, they create their own version of the information.

I have been involved with businesses that have similar information in multiple formats or spreadsheets. People can sometimes build silos of their own data and information because they need it in a slightly different format.

Having this kind of scenario may derail your business.

Once your systems are created, they must be written down in a procedures manual.

This is important for a couple reasons.

First, by having them in writing, you can use the manual as a tool in training your people and for accountability purposes.

Second, by having a procedures manual or "operations manual", your business' value increases. Any time a new owner is provided a "systemized" approach to running your business, it is more valuable to that person than buying a business and then having to figure out how to operate it.

Do you have systems and processes that you can count on and that are not replicated in multiple formats?

Do you have a centralized database of information that every employee is required to utilize?

You have systems and processes in place and have them well documented. Everyone is able to use them effectively and efficiently. The information is accessed on a regular basis and your staff is able to provide the information you need to run the business.

When your systems and processes are documented, your people need to be trained (or re-trained) so everyone knows what the procedures are and understands how to follow those procedures.

Everyone needs to be held accountable to following the procedures at all times and to be continuously on the lookout for opportunities to improve the procedures.

How well documented are your systems and processes? If an employee were let go, would someone else be able to take over the responsibilities and follow the process or system?

You feel confident that someone else could take over, but will they be able to follow the same methods?

Many times when someone is replaced the new employee has his or her own ideas of how a process or system should work. They may base their ideas on a prior position they held with a previous business.

They may have some good ideas but they may not fit your culture or business environment.

Have checks and balances in place so that you will know when a system or process isn't working or isn't being followed.

Be confident that people are not creating their own processes and systems that are outside of the business principles. Have values that are reflected in your systems and processes so that everyone knows how you do business. Your customers or clients are confident in your business providing them products and services they can count on because you provide them information that is accurate. Your suppliers and vendors appreciate the information you provide them so that they can run their business effectively and fulfill your needs in a timely manner.

If you want to dramatically increase your profits, identifying and plugging the many little profit holes in your company will help you greatly.

If your business is currently not profitable, then this is a great place to begin to turn that around. Some of the profit holes can be related to a lack of systems and processes.

There is place you can look to find every single profit hole in your company. That place is your company's income statement (profit and loss statement, also called your P&L). If you can read your company's P&L detail report, you'll see where every single dollar comes in and goes out of your business. If you don't have the ability to do that, you need to change that immediately.

Having a good understanding of your financial statements is critical to running any business. You may need someone to interpret them for you like an accountant, but you need to learn how to do this yourself.

Create an executive dashboard for your business that gives you a snapshot of your business so that you can easily get the pulse of the business on a regular basis even when you are not present at one of your locations, if there is more than one.

Be able to access the dashboard when you are out of the office or traveling. Be confident that the information is accurate and you don't have to just go with your gut feel for where the business is at financially.

The information provides you with Key Performance Indicators (KPIs) for your business so that you can make key decisions.

As the business owner, it isn't your job to create the systems yourself. It isn't your responsibility to document the systems and create a procedural manual. But it is ultimately your responsibility to make sure that they get done appropriately.

Don't be overwhelmed if you currently don't have any written systems in your business or if your systems have become stale. Just work with your people to create a list of systems that need to be created or updated and then prioritize the list.

Once that's done, you can start knocking them out one by one. It won't happen overnight, but that's okay. Remember the question is "How do you eat an elephant?" Answer is: "One bite at a time." The same is true with creating your business operations manual. "How do you create your operations manual?" Answer is: "One system at a time."

There are strategic partners that you engage with on a regular basis, which help to have another set of eyes looking at your business from an outside perspective. They are a sounding board you can go to for a different perspective or to bounce ideas off of.

They are looking out for your best interest and not how it may affect their business. Your partners share some of the same values so that they are able to relate to your culture or views.

They periodically challenge you as a business owner or manager to think outside of the box. They may have some similar processes and systems in their business. They help you to see the forest for the trees.

Do you have a specific process and sales story for why your business is different?

Having a sales process allows you to qualify prospects before investing time in marketing to them and trying to build a relationship. Your sales process can include demographics, psychographics, and other criteria. You may be looking for consumers or businesses in a certain geographic area.

What particular characteristics do they have in common?

For business-to-business sales you may want a certain size business based on number of employees, revenue per year, type of business, growth potential, specific industry, or other criteria.

Does the business utilize your types of products or services?

Identify the prospects challenges and how your solution addresses them. Spend time to understand if the prospect actually fits your selection criteria. Interview the prospect once you have pre-qualified them in order to determine it is a good fit for you and for them. Have some tools that enable you to provide the best solution for their needs. These tools may include a process for analyzing their real need.

Do their wants actually meet their specific needs?

When you don't get the sale, try to determine why so that you learn from it and are able to address any objections that caused you not to get the sale. Price is usually not the real reason, even though the prospect may say it was. Try to dig a little deeper. They may have made up their mind before you actually met with them.
Take time to educate your current customers and clients on the products and services you offer.

I recall when I was running one of my Information Technology businesses that I would find out that a client had purchased a particular piece of equipment that we could have supplied. They bought it because they did not know we could provide it. That was a lesson learned!

Do you have a consistent marketing process?

Your marketing process needs to include a marketing calendar for consistent initiatives in a timely manner. You probably would not market snowmobiles in April in Minnesota.

Know what the cycles are for your business. When do your prospects look for your type of products or services? What is a trigger that gets them interested?

Have a call to action on all your materials and points of contact. Have something of value to give away, but is must be valuable to them.

Do not make your marketing information to technical unless it is to be given to a technical contact.

Many people are not looking for all the details, but they are looking for how it benefits them.

The old saying is that they want to know **"What's in it for me" (WIIFM).** Use various methods to educate your target audience on a consistent basis. Follow up on leads and referrals in a timely manner.

If your sales are flat, don't just assume that it is a marketing issue.

It may be a sales, customer service, or follow up issue. What is your new customer or client acquisition rate or conversion rate?

What is your customer or client retention rate? What is your average purchase amount? What is your gross margin and profit margin?

Consistently evaluate these areas of your business and keep a scorecard on a periodic basis.

Try to make the marketing and sales information easy to understand.

I attended a marketing seminar where we were asked to create an audio logo for our business. Each person read his or her statement to another person. Many of the statements were very confusing and included jargon like, I work with people who need constant comprehensive methodical adjustments in order to alleviate their excruciating pain and frustration.

What does that mean?

Your audio logo or meme needs to be simple and short. A window cleaner may say, "I take the pane out of cleaning windows". A lawn service may say "I make the grass greener on your side of the fence". A jeweler may say, "We make diamonds sparkle".

You get the idea.

Do you have a script(s) that you follow when you attend a networking event or when someone asks you what you do? Others in your business are able to repeat it so that everyone in the business has a clear understanding of what the business provides.

I have attended many networking events where people stumble over what to say or they are constantly changing it.

Have your sales pitch be a conversation, instead of trying to convince someone that they need to buy your products or services.

Give them a sample of what it is like to work with your business.

Have some case studies of how your products or services helped a client or customer. The case studies need to have some quotes from the client or customer in their own words.

You may have to create a case study or testimonial together for them to sign off on.

You can also have it created on their letterhead or with their logo.

Have a website with your own domain name not a generic one. Also have an email address that is not a free service like Gmail.

Have business cards and other materials that are not from a free service or looks like many others.

What systems and processes can you improve on?

Are all your systems and processes functioning at their peak?

All Systems Go!

Know Destination

"If I had nine hours to chop down a tree, I would spend the first six sharpening my axe." - *Abraham Lincoln*

"Always focus on the front windshield and not the rearview mirror." - *Colin Powell*

Do you know where your business is heading?

Is it in the right direction?

Do you know your final destination and how you are going to get there? Do you have specific measurable goals and objectives to meet in a certain time frame?

You have your path all mapped out and know how you are going to follow it. It is said the people who fail to plan, plan to fail.

You have a business plan, which includes a marketing plan but it is sitting on a shelf. Periodically review it, as many business owners have not since it was created.

Understand that it may need some changes as your business grows. Many people just don't seem to have the time to deal with it.

Someone told you that you need a business plan and they wrote it for you. Maybe you thought that was a great idea since you did not know what a business plan is or how to go about writing one.

They put their ideas about your business into the plan. They completed the plan and presented it to you and you thought you would never have to look at it again. A business plan needs to be written by the business owners with his or her owns words and ideas for the business. It is YOUR business not theirs.

If you were going on a vacation you would first plan your final destination and your stops along the way. You would plan how you will get to your destination (methods). You determine if you have enough money to reach your destination. You include others in your planning so that they are all on board with it. You make sure you have all the supplies you need to get to your destination. After all how many people take a vacation with no planning or destination in mind?

There will be times when you set out in a specific direction, however, new things come up that you may not have foreseen, or new information becomes available. It's important to know when to implement changes to get back on track. This can be compared to detours on a railroad when you are moving towards a destination.

Sometimes you have to switch tracks in order to avoid areas that are under construction. You may not have expected the detour, however, it's there and you have to deal with it. So follow the new route, go around, make adjustments and get back on track.

No Plan = No Destination, Know Plan = Know Destination.

"Vision" then "Strategy" then "Tactics" then "Action steps to take this week". In other words, know where you are going, have a plan to get there, break the plan down into initiatives, and then break the initiatives down into specific tasks you will complete this week. Development is a step-by-step process of forward movement. This is an undeniable fact.

I know what you feel like, as I have owned businesses related to my education as an Information Technology consultant. I provided IT services to clients for over 30 years and was never trained on running a business.

I developed my own accounting systems to run the business and was the person in charge of all of the financial information for the businesses. I interacted with the suppliers of products we sold to our clients, tracked the payables, billed the clients, received the payments, secured loans if needed, set up lease payments, and the list goes on.

I spent a majority of my time IN the business and very little time planning the direction of the business.

I learned it the hard way. Therefore, you can reap the rewards of my experience of being a business owner and knowing some of the issues and struggles that you face every day.

What are your issues and struggles that you are dealing with?

I can relate.

You are a lot like I was. You spend a majority of your time IN the business and less time ON the business.

Spending time ON the business is strategic to a healthy and growing business.

Take some time at least annually to get away from the daily grind and to think about your business direction and initiatives. When you return to the business, nothing much seems to change as you get back to the daily issues and struggles.

It is hard to take action on the ideas that you planned at the annual strategy session. You just don't seem to find the time to address the actions that need to be taken.

When will you have the time?

This is where you can utilize the confidential advice or just a listening ear of a certified professional business advisor or coach. By having consistent action steps that you are held accountable to achieve, your business will keep moving forward. Before you know it, you will reach your destination. We can help YOU get there.

You can focus on the past and be stagnant with your business endeavor or you can look to the future destination of where your business is heading. You may change your destination but you always need to have a map to follow.

Using the three L's you can:

- **Learn** from the past – utilize what you have learned to move your business forward and transform it into the future by developing a plan of action.

- **Live** in the present – be all in (present) as your business grows since you can't change the past but you can create a future path for your business.

- **Look** to the future – paint a picture of what your business can be like in the future. Have a clear picture so that you and others can visualize where the business is going.

"Learn from the past, prepare for the future, and perform in the moment." - **Mike Van Hoozer**

Know Plan, Know Destination

Stop at the Depot

"Dream as if you'll live forever, live as if you'll die tomorrow." - *Author unknown*

"You must live in the present, launch yourself on every wave, find your eternity in each moment." - *Henry David Thoreau*

Take the time to reevaluate the business and step back and reflect on your direction. Take some time away from the business to strategize about the future.

Where is the business heading? Is it the right direction?

What is working, not working, needs to be corrected, or is too complicated?

Engage with your team and advisors in order to discover any issues that have been lurking in the background and need some attention.

When was the last time you spent some valuable time ON the business?

Find a place to get away from all of the daily interruptions or distractions to focus on your business.

You need to bring clarity to your business endeavors.

What will the next year, 3 years, or 5 years look like?

Create a plan for how you are going to get there.

Will your business require additional funds, people, resources, outside services, etc.?

Is your business supporting you or are you supporting your business?

It is time to address your business strategies and functions.

If you don't, who will?

I remember times in businesses that I have owned or worked for in which I had been struggling to find a solution to an issue I was having. I would continue for a time trying to determine what I needed to do. Finally, I decided to leave it alone for a while maybe overnight or a day later. Many times the solution would hit me in the middle of the night or when I next looked at the issue. I don't always know how but by putting it aside the solution came to me.

Sometimes just getting away to another task will give you insight into the solution for another issue.

The depot is the place where can assemble the plan in order for your troops (employees) to carry out the plan.

It is also the place to work on maintaining your business so that it function more efficiently and effectively. It can also be the place that you as the owner are able to recharge. Who doesn't need to reflect on where they are and where they are going?

If not, you must be going nowhere.

What is your dream for the business?

When we stop and listen, we are able to see more clearly where we are headed and if it is the direction we really want to go.

Have you ever been traveling somewhere you have already been and all of the sudden realize that you took a wrong turn?

You feel lost until you see something you recognize and you get a clear picture of what direction to turn.

This is also a time to reflect on what is working, not working, needs to be fixed, or is confusing.

Do you have issues that consistently raise their ugly head?

What needs to change?

Celebrate your accomplishments regularly. We tend to forget what we have accomplished until we stop and reflect.

What do you want to accomplish next?

You may stop to reflect on your To Do list, but what about your Not To Do list. Your Not To Do list is all the tasks and projects that really should not be on your list.

Do you spend time taking on tasks that someone else could be doing?

If you are like others, or even me you may be checking your email too frequently, answering unnecessary phone calls, jumping into issues someone else could solve.

I remember having a boss a number of years ago that would hear that a customer had an issue. He found out that I was working on it. He proceeded to find me and ask if I knew how to fix the issue. I got frustrated and told him that if he left me alone I would be able to solve it. I had the issue resolved in less than 5 minutes.

Sometimes you have to trust your employees with developing the solution.

Do not spend your time reflecting on what could have or should have happened in the past, but focus your efforts on moving forward. This will help you to be more productive, successful, and will build your business much faster.

Don't wait until everything is perfect to move ahead. Just keep at it one step at a time.

Contemplate some ideas for how you might engage your target audience.

You may decide to sponsor an event in order promote your business brand. You will want to choose events where your prospects would be.

A manufacturer may sponsor a golf tournament that is attending by others in a particular association.

A massage therapist may want to provide free massages at an event where people are tense or stressed out.

You can also allow your employees to take time to reflect. Very few companies give their employees time for reflection, especially when competitive pressures are escalating.

Usually the imperative is to double down and work harder, don't stop to think, just drive forward. There is value in time for reflection, in that it helps people to do a better job.

As we think about the depot, it can also be a place (station) where you can stock up on the necessary supplies you need to continue in the business.

In other words, keep a supply of materials like books, videos, and others that will help you to gain more knowledge, education, and understanding about running a business. Create a space with a library or publications that stimulate your mind. Some people meditate on what they read or view in order to comprehend it more. Some people like to listen to audio while they drive to a particular location. Whatever helps you to concentrate on the next steps you need to take ACTION on.

If you always do what you have always done, you will always get what you have already got.

In Conclusion

"I insist on a lot of time being spent, almost every day, to just sit and think. That is very uncommon in American business. I read and think. So I do more reading and thinking, and make less impulse decisions than most people in business. I do it because I like this kind of life." - *Warren Buffet*

"I used to use business to make money. But I've learned that business is a tool. You can use it to support what you believe in." - *Po Bronson*

I want to congratulate you on reaching the end of the book.

I hope that you were able to gain some insight into some of the issues that many business owners and managers have to deal with.

Being a business owner or manager has its rewards and benefits but it does require commitment and strategy in order to keep an eye on the details (from a distance) and Soar above the crowd!

We can help you to move your business to the next stage.

In order to move your business forward, you need to continue to educate yourself on running your business more effectively and efficiently.

They say that the biggest room in a business is the room for improvement.

The next question is **"When will you take action?"**

Remember in the introduction of this book that we addressed **Education + Application = Wisdom**.

Education is gaining the knowledge and understanding, but without application of the education it is futile. You need to take deliberate action steps in order to move your business forward.

Nothing stays the same but there is also nothing new under the sun.

What actions will you take to move your business to the next stage?

To be honest many business owners and managers will not take much, if any action at all.

This is where the metal meets the rail.

You have to do something different in order to see your business **SOAR**.

In working with business owners and managers I have seen them struggle with the same issues regularly. You are the only one who can make a difference in your own business by taking action.

When others see you taking action they will get on board and follow your lead.

The pace of everyday life many times gets in the way and we procrastinate or just neglect to do something. We get tied up in the daily activities and lose sight of our goals and objectives. We have very little time to spend on the business strategies. We tend to think that issues will just disappear or we hope they will.

Change is hard work but it is beneficial to your growth as a person and as a business.

We make business objectives and goals with the same mindset we use for New Year's Resolutions.
We all know how long resolutions last, right?

Resolutions seem to last a couple of weeks or months or until we just forget about them. We see it all the time. It is common.

There are a small percentage of people that attend seminars or read a book like this that actually take action on what they have learned. They take the information and file it somewhere until they find it again and determine that they no longer need it.

I have read many books and attended seminars where I have had the same experience.

What do we remember the most? We remember those things that we repeat. We remember what we actually put into action or what we can visualize.

Make the action a habit and you will continue to take the action.

Without having a clear plan of action, support, and accountability you will find that you will forget what you learn from this book or how you can utilize it. You will not implement much or any of the basic business ideas I have shared with you.

It is very possible that a number of the issues and topics that I have shared in this book resonate with you.

Did you see yourself in any specific areas?

How will you address these areas of your business?

Where will you start and when will you take action?

There are key areas of your business that need to be examined and require your immediate attention. You need to take the most urgent first and have a focus on one area at a time.

You have a large endeavor in order to make your business soar, but you need to look at it in bite sized pieces.

You can only eat an elephant one small bite at a time.

In my businesses, I relied on my own understanding and did not seek the advice of other business professionals. I thought that I knew all that I needed to know in order to run a business.

I rarely had time to read a book like this or even spend the time to find information on making the business better. I would listen to the advice of friends, family, or others who have never ran a business. Many people can give you advice, but is it good or the right advice?

This is where an advance certified business advisor or coach can help you to reach your goals and objectives. They can help you to narrow down the area to focus on. They will help you to create specific action steps that you need to take. They can keep you accountable to fulfilling your actions. They will help you develop clear action steps that are attainable and that will transform your business.

A lot of business people and executives are looking to retain the services of a business advisor or coach because of the many benefits they provide. While you may hire an advisor or coach to help you with a particular issue or problem, you may want to become more productive, motivated, or forward thinking. Let us focus in on a few of the benefits of getting your own advisor or coach.

Having a business advisor or coach is an excellent way to help you be motivated and dedicated to what you want to achieve.

This is incredibly helpful for a new entrepreneur who may have spent the majority of their career working for others.

You don't have a boss or administrator to turn to for help, so it can be extremely helpful to have someone to talk to that can relate to your issues. The advisor or coach is somebody who can help you define your goals, overcome issues, and allow you to see things more clearly.

If you ever feel overwhelmed or distressed about something, they can give you some assistance and enable you to put things into perspective.

The need to have reassurance and motivation from people is vital and a good advisor or coach is skilled at providing that at the proper time. He or she will actively listen to your concerns and help you to prioritize the list of actions to take.

An advanced certified business coach is a person who can help you to brainstorm new concepts.
You can easily get into a mental rut where you have a tough time determining new solutions. Doing the same things the same old way isn't necessarily productive, and occasionally it can be catastrophic.

The coach will help you identify new possibilities and systems. He or she isn't really there to carry out your work for you, but to help you discover better ways of doing it yourself.

If the person has a great deal of experience, they will be able to help you come up with different ways to do a task. Having someone to help you think of productive ideas is one of the main benefits of business coaching.

The advisor or coach is one who could see you and your business objectively, from the outside.

It is very easy to miss particular information if you spend your time on the inside, so they can point out things that you may not have noticed.

You'll find that a particular process in your business may not be as efficient as it ought to be. But as this is the way in which it was always done, you may not see other options as being better.

However, your business coach will see the inefficiencies in your business and can point them out to you. By being an impartial observer, they can provide a valuable point of view that can help your business in many ways.

These are a few of the reasons why there is an increase in interest to work with business coaches. The assistance and direction a business coach gives can help you fix a lot of issues in your business. That is why coaching will benefit you in more ways than you can even predict, and it can be a good investment in your business's future.

Your advisor or coach has experience in running a business. They have strategies, tools, training, and support to keep you on track. They will help your business to not become derailed along the way but to stay on track.

My goal is to help you and your business to SOAR and get the results that you desire for your business as we take it one step at a time. You and your business have spent some amount of time to get where you are today. It will also take some time to move your business from where it is to where you want it to be.

"I absolutely believe that people, unless coached, never reach their maximum capabilities." - *Bob Nardelli, former CEO, Home Depot*

"A coach is part advisor, part sounding board, part cheerleader, part manager and part strategist." *The Business Journal*

"I never cease to be amazed at the power of the coaching process to draw out the skills or talent that was previously hidden within an individual, and which invariably finds a way to solve a problem previously thought unsolvable."
John Russell, Managing Director, Harley-Davidson Europe Ltd.

"Coaching is an action-oriented partnership that, unlike psychotherapy which delves into patterns of the past, concentrates on where you are today and how you can reach your goals."*Time*

"If you want to build your business and at the same time have a rewarding personal life, you call a coach."***Robert Schwab, 'Businesses Hire Coaches to Build Winning Teams,' Denver Post***

"Many of the World's most admired corporations, from GE to Goldman Sachs, invest in coaching. Annual spending on coaching in the US is estimated at roughly $1 Billion Dollars."***Harvard Business Review***

Watch for all of our books on Amazon at
www.amazon.com

Check out our resources on our website.

You can contact Soaring Eagles Business Advisors via

www.soaringeaglesba.com **or**

email to: mailto:info@soaringeaglesba.com

It will be the best decision you have made in moving your business to soaring above the crowd!

We Transform Business.

Transform your business and not be derailed!

About Soaring Eagles Business Advisors

We are dedicated to helping business owners and managers to build their business from startup to soaring. We build a relationship with those we serve. We look to the best interests of our clients and how we can best serve them. We are committed to helping our clients achieve their goals and objectives in their business and quality of life.

We strive to keep our education and actions current so that we can better serve our clients. We are constantly looking at tools and strategies in order to improve our business.

We have an extensive network of other business professionals that we can leverage in order to benefit our clients.

We provide initial evaluations as to your business health and your work and life balance.

We believe that personal and business effectiveness are directly linked.
We help business owners and managers to discover what behaviors may be holding them back. We help business owners and managers to look at themselves in the mirror and to reflect on their effectiveness.

We focus on each client specifically, which allows us to meet his or her specific needs.

We are an independent business and do not have a cookie cutter approach to helping business owners and managers.

We also have been a business owner or manager in order to be able to relate to the challenges you face.

We are qualified to assist you with your unique business issues.

About Steven J. Beaman

Steven works with the business owner or manager to help them achieve their goals and objectives. He helps them to determine what specific actions they need to take. He uses active listening techniques to connect with a business owner or manager in order to provide them direction, advice, consultative, or technical knowledge.

Steven has owned businesses for over 30 years. He has been an owner of Information technology businesses that helped many types of businesses to create processes and systems that eliminate redundancy and inefficiencies.

He has created systems in the accounting, manufacturing, distribution, retail, and service industries.

Thank you for reading this book and we wish you the best in your business.

www.ingramcontent.com/pod-product-compliance
Lightning Source LLC
Chambersburg PA
CBHW060031210326
41520CB00009B/1078